DID YOU SEE THAT DINOSAUR?

Interior and Cover Designers: Eric Pratt and Angie Chiu
Art Producer: Sue Bischofberger
Editor: Erin Nelson
Production Managers: Oriana Siska and Riley Hoffman
Production Editor: Erum Khan

Illustration © 2020 Scott Koblish. Colors by Monica Kubina.
Artist photo courtesy of Jillian Adams.

ISBN: Print 978-1-64152-706-4
R0

DID YOU SEE THAT DINOSAUR?

SEARCH THE PAGE, FIND THE DINOSAUR IN A FACT-FILLED ADVENTURE

RILEY BLACK

Illustrations by Scott Koblish

R

ROCKRIDGE
PRESS

To Splash
Let's find dinosaurs together.

A NOTE TO PARENTS

The world is full of wonders. The trick is finding them all.

Search-and-find books help children engage with what they see—from big to small, and even through time. In an age of so much distraction, search-and-finds help young readers cultivate focus and attention to detail—habits they'll carry with them throughout their lives.

But this book isn't just about finding dinosaurs. The activities here also help foster pattern-seeking, making small details jump into focus. Educational text rewards young readers with in-depth knowledge of the natural world.

The dinosaurs and other prehistoric creatures in this book are certainly whimsical. They are literal rock stars, famous to paleontologists and children in all of their winged, clawed, and fanged glory. Each animal is accompanied by facts about its life and environment, generated from decades of scientific study. This book even includes new discoveries never illustrated before.

By paying close attention to these animals in their natural habitats, children are likely to remember the details. What's more, the dinosaurs here are an invitation for children to learn, explore, and—with the help of a little time travel—tap into the majesty of their own imaginations.

TRIASSIC

252 TO 201
MILLION YEARS AGO

PLATEOSAURUS
214 to 204 million years ago

JURASSIC

201 TO 145
MILLION YEARS AGO

DILOPHOSAURUS
200 to 193 million years ago

PLESIOSAURUS
198 to 175 million years ago

CRETACEOUS

145 TO 66
MILLION YEARS AGO

OURANOSAURUS
125 to 112 million years ago

UTAHRAPTOR
126 million years ago

VELOCIRAPTOR
75 to 71 million years ago

TAWA
215 to 213 million years ago

CAELESTIVENTUS
210 to 200 million years ago

MEGALOSAURUS
166 million years ago

STEGOSAURUS
155 to 148 million years ago

BRACHIOSAURUS
154 to 153 million years ago

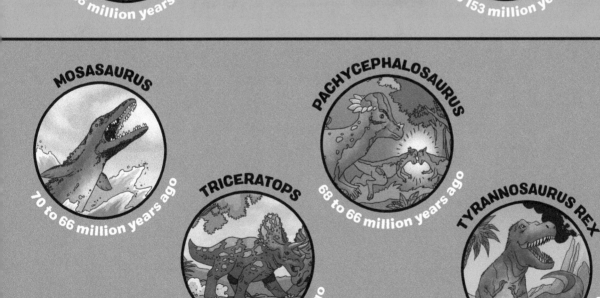

MOSASAURUS
70 to 66 million years ago

TRICERATOPS
68 to 66 million years ago

PACHYCEPHALOSAURUS
68 to 66 million years ago

TYRANNOSAURUS REX
68 to 66 million years ago

DID YOU SEE THAT DINOSAUR?

Maybe you have seen one at a museum. You can see a lot of old bones there. But what about a real, living dinosaur? That's who Ava and Mateo want to meet. They're two kids just like you, and they want to grow up to be paleontologists someday. A paleontologist is a scientist who studies plants and animals that lived a long, long time ago.

Dinosaurs were reptiles, but different from the lizards, snakes, and turtles alive today. Some had very long necks and tails and grew to be more than 100 feet long. That's longer than two school buses! Others walked on two legs and had smiles full of sharp teeth.

Most of our favorite dinosaurs lived millions of years ago, so how do paleontologists know about all these dinosaurs? Fossils. Fossils are impressions of creatures, usually in rocks, left behind a long time ago. How amazing would it be to see, hear, and even smell some of our favorite dinosaurs? That's just what Ava and Mateo are going to do, and they want you to go with them! They've got some special help from a time machine set to travel to the wonderful Age of Dinosaurs—the Mesozoic Era.

Dinosaurs can be hard to find, though. You'll have to work with Ava and Mateo as a dinosaur spotter to help them on their expedition!

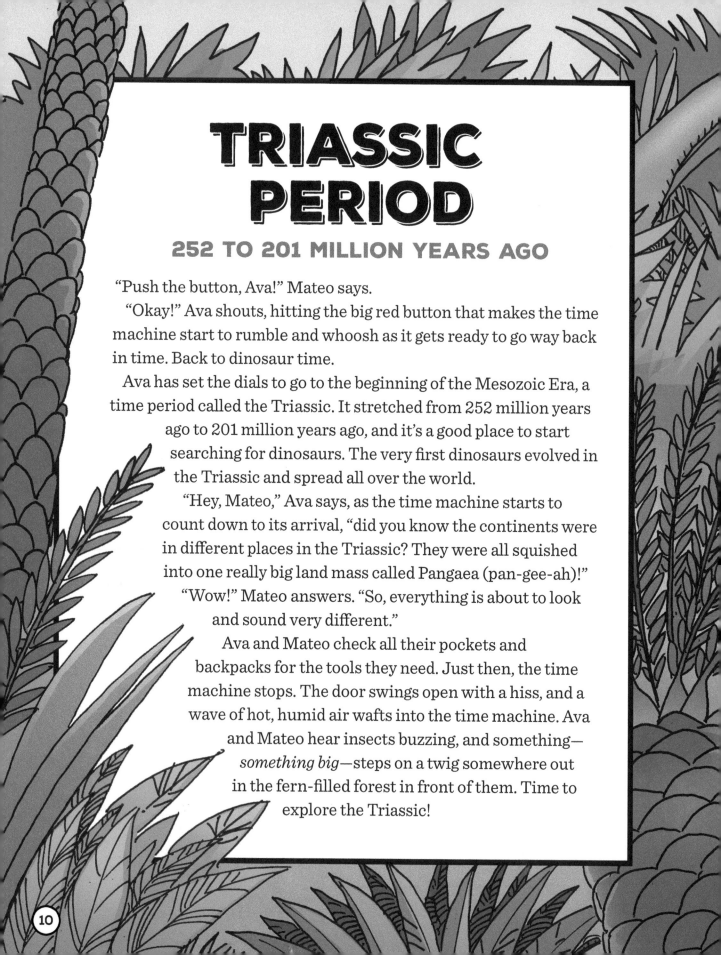

TRIASSIC PERIOD

252 TO 201 MILLION YEARS AGO

"Push the button, Ava!" Mateo says.

"Okay!" Ava shouts, hitting the big red button that makes the time machine start to rumble and whoosh as it gets ready to go way back in time. Back to dinosaur time.

Ava has set the dials to go to the beginning of the Mesozoic Era, a time period called the Triassic. It stretched from 252 million years ago to 201 million years ago, and it's a good place to start searching for dinosaurs. The very first dinosaurs evolved in the Triassic and spread all over the world.

"Hey, Mateo," Ava says, as the time machine starts to count down to its arrival, "did you know the continents were in different places in the Triassic? They were all squished into one really big land mass called Pangaea (pan-gee-ah)!"

"Wow!" Mateo answers. "So, everything is about to look and sound very different."

Ava and Mateo check all their pockets and backpacks for the tools they need. Just then, the time machine stops. The door swings open with a hiss, and a wave of hot, humid air wafts into the time machine. Ava and Mateo hear insects buzzing, and something—*something big*—steps on a twig somewhere out in the fern-filled forest in front of them. Time to explore the Triassic!

PLATEOSAURUS

(play-tee-oh-sawr-us)

214 TO 204 MILLION YEARS AGO

Food: **Herbivore** • Size: **Up to 30 feet long**
Family: **Sauropodomorpha** • Home: **Prehistoric Germany and Greenland**

"Whoa!" Mateo says. "It sure is hot!"

"The Triassic is warmer than when we're from," Ava says. "There isn't even ice at the poles!"

"But where are we now?" Mateo asks.

"We're in prehistoric Germany," Ava says. "That's where the *Plateosaurus* lives!"

Ava and Mateo take out their binoculars. There sure are a lot of plants. There are ferns and a plant called a cycad that looks like a big pineapple.

"There!" Mateo exclaims. With a deep rumble, a dinosaur steps into view. "*Plateosaurus*! How big do you think it is?"

"I think this one's about 16 feet long," Ava says, "but some of them get bigger."

"Look at that neck!" Mateo gasps. "And the tiny head."

"*Plateosaurus* most likely used that long neck to reach high into the trees for food," Ava says, "and that long tail for balance because it walked on two legs."

"Those claws are pretty cool, too," Mateo says. "Maybe those helped scare predators away?"

"Those claw hugs must hurt!" Ava laughs.

HOW MANY OF THE SEARCH ITEMS CAN YOU FIND?

1. rock hammer
2. map
3. *Plateosaurus* claw
4. canteen
5. watch
6. notebook
7. compass
8. insect-chewed leaves

TAWA

(ta-wah)

215 TO 213 MILLION YEARS AGO

Food: Carnivore • Size: 8 feet long • Family: Theropoda
Home: Prehistoric North America, in what is now New Mexico

A small, pointy head pokes out of the forest.

"I wonder what kind of dinosaur that is," Mateo says.

"I think it's a *Tawa*," Ava whispers. Just then, the dinosaur hops out of the forest, shaking dewdrops from the ferns. "Yes, it's a *Tawa*! Its name comes from a Hopi word for a sun god."

"Does that mean it comes from New Mexico?" Mateo asks.

"That's right!" Ava says. "Its bones were found in a place called Ghost Ranch."

The dinosaur moves closer, trotting on two legs toward Ava and Mateo.

"I think it's getting closer, Ava," Mateo whispers. "Is it a dangerous dinosaur?"

"*Tawa* is a carnivore, but it eats smaller things like lizards," Ava explains. "We're too big."

"That's right!" Mateo says.

"*Tawa* is just the beginning of a dinosaur family. See, it's just a shrimposaurus," Ava jokes.

HOW MANY OF THE SEARCH ITEMS CAN YOU FIND?

1. *Tawa* tailbone
2. radio
3. awl
4. time machine key
5. magnifying glass
6. hand lens

CAELESTIVENTUS

(say-lest-ee-vent-us)

210 TO 200 MILLION YEARS AGO

Food: Insectivore • **Size:** 4 feet wide • **Family:** Pterosaur
Home: Prehistoric North America, in what is now Utah

Skreek! A shadow passes over Ava and Mateo. They look up to see a creature flying above the sandy desert. They're in ancient Utah 200 million years ago!

"What is that?" Ava says, squinting to see the animal.

"That's a *Caelestiventus*!" Mateo says, jumping up and down. "Its name means 'heavenly wind.'"

"It looks kind of scary, though," Ava says. "Look at all those teeth!"

"Back in the Triassic, all the pterosaurs still had teeth," Mateo says. "They used them to catch bugs and other little snacks."

"But it's not a dinosaur, right?" Ava asks.

"Right!" Mateo says. "Pterosaurs are cousins of dinosaurs, and they lived at the same time, but they belong to a totally different family. You can always tell them apart by their leathery wings. They're made of skin stretched between their bodies and a long, long finger. Look at it swoop!"

The *Caelestiventus* dives through the air and snaps its jaws, grabbing a dragonfly.

HOW MANY OF THE SEARCH ITEMS CAN YOU FIND?

1. fossil brush
2. *Caelestiventus* skull
3. hand lens
4. canteen
5. magnifying glass
6. crocodile

JURASSIC PERIOD

201 TO 145 MILLION YEARS AGO

"We saw some pretty big dinosaurs in the Triassic, like *Plateosaurus,*" Ava says.

"But in the Jurassic, dinosaurs get really, super, amazingly big!" Mateo replies, watching the time ticker bring them to the Jurassic.

Ava watches the temperature gauge shift as the time machine gets closer to the start of the Jurassic. Then she remembers, "Hey, the continents are going to be in different shapes!"

"Why is that?" Mateo asks, watching the monitors get warmer.

"It's called continental drift," Ava says. "The continents are on plates that move around very, very slowly. In the Jurassic, Pangaea breaks apart into two halves. There's a supercontinent called Laurasia in the north part of the world and one called Gondwana in the south. Which do you want to visit first?"

"Laurasia!" Mateo exclaims. "That's where some of my favorite dinosaurs are!" And just like that, the time machine lights blink green, welcoming Ava and Mateo to the Jurassic.

DILOPHOSAURUS

(die-low-pho-sawr-us)

200 TO 193 MILLION YEARS AGO

Food: Carnivore • **Size:** 23 feet long • **Family:** Theropoda
Home: The first bones were found on a Navajo Indian Reservation in Arizona

Ava and Mateo walk around the edge of a prehistoric lake following big three-toed tracks in the mud.

"Are you sure we're in the Jurassic?" Mateo asks. "These tracks look like they were made by a big chicken."

Ava laughs. "I'm sure! The coordinates say we're in prehistoric Arizona, about 200 million years ago. There were never chickens this big. These were probably made by *Dilophosaurus*."

Mateo takes out his binoculars and looks at the other side of the lake.

A large shape walks along the shore, bobbing its head like a bird.

"There!" Mateo says. "The *Dilophosaurus*! Its name means 'two-crested lizard' for the delicate ornaments on its head."

"Its teeth sure look sharp," Ava says. "What do you think it eats?"

"Maybe we can find out if we watch," Mateo whispers.

The *Dilophosaurus* pauses at the edge of the lake and stands very still. All of a sudden—*snap!* It ducks its head into the water and comes up with a wriggling fish.

HOW MANY OF THE SEARCH ITEMS CAN YOU FIND?

1. binoculars
2. notebook
3. *Dilophosaurus* tooth
4. watch
5. compass
6. canteen

PLESIOSAURUS

(plee-see-oh-sawr-us)

198 TO 175 MILLION YEARS AGO

Food: Piscivore • Size: 10 feet long • Family: Plesiosauria
Home: Tethys Sea, off the southern coast of prehistoric England

"I wish I had brought my swimsuit!" Ava says, standing on the Jurassic beach.

Just then, a shadow glides through the waves. A long neck with a tiny head rises above the surface. The reptile snorts saltwater out of its nostrils and goes back underwater, paddling its big flippers.

"A *Plesiosaurus*!" Mateo shouts.

"But this isn't a dinosaur, right?" Ava asks.

"That's right," Mateo replies. "The *Plesiosaurus* belongs to a great big family of reptiles that are different from dinosaurs. They evolved to live in the oceans at the same time the dinosaurs were on land."

Ava checks their coordinates. She and Mateo are in prehistoric England. "Do *Plesiosaurus* only live here?" she asks.

"*Plesiosaurus* lived for tens of millions of years, all over the world," Mateo says, "even in Antarctica!"

Right then, the *Plesiosaurus* changes direction and darts through the waves, making tiny silvery fish jump out of the water.

"I think it's hunting!" Ava adds.

"I think I'll stay on the beach today," Mateo says.

HOW MANY OF THE SEARCH ITEMS CAN YOU FIND?

1. binoculars
2. watch
3. notebook
4. compass
5. rock hammer
6. map

MEGALOSAURUS

(meg-ah-low-sawr-us)

166 MILLION YEARS AGO

Food: Carnivore • Size: 30 feet long • Family: Theropoda
Home: Prehistoric southern England

"I can't believe we get to see a *Megalosaurus*!" Ava says.

The carnivorous dinosaur strides through the forest on powerful hind legs. It stops to sniff the air.

"This is the first dinosaur to ever get named, right?" Mateo asks.

"Right!" Ava says. "Even though people had been finding dinosaur bones for hundreds of years, *Megalosaurus* was the first one to get a scientific name. Its name means 'great lizard.'"

The dinosaur strides forward again, clenching and unclenching its claws.

Mateo tilts his head. "It doesn't look much like a lizard to me. Why did they name it that?"

"Most dinosaur skeletons aren't complete," Ava says. "Back then, all experts had was a piece of jaw and some other bones, so they thought it was a big reptile, like a crocodile. Better skeletons changed the picture."

"Imagine if they could see this!" Mateo says.

The carnivore snorts and runs deeper into the woods. Dinner time!

HOW MANY OF THE SEARCH ITEMS CAN YOU FIND?

1. watch
2. notebook
3. *Megalosaurus* claw
4. binoculars
5. rock hammer
6. map
7. compass

STEGOSAURUS

(steg-oh-sawr-us)

155 TO 148 MILLION YEARS AGO

Food: Herbivore • **Size:** 30 feet long • **Family:** Stegosauridae
Home: Prehistoric North America, in what is now Utah, Colorado, and Wyoming

"Now that is a prickly dinosaur," Mateo says as they watch the *Stegosaurus* walk slowly near a riverbank. The dinosaur's tail gently sways. At the end of the tail are four spikes.

"Why do you think it's so pointy?" Ava asks.

"You know, scientists have been wondering that for a long time," Mateo says.

Looking closer, Mateo and Ava can see that the underside of the dinosaur's throat is covered with pebble-like armor called osteoderms. Along the dinosaur's back are big triangular plates.

"I think the neck armor and spikes are to protect it from powerful carnivores," Mateo says.

"But what about those funky plates?" Ava asks. "I don't think they're for serving dinner."

"Scientists used to think that they helped the dinosaur warm up in the morning," Mateo says. "But now, experts think the plates were a way for *Stegosauruses* to talk to each other."

With a loud bellow, another *Stegosaurus* steps out into the clearing. Ava looks at Mateo. "Maybe it wants to chat?"

HOW MANY OF THE SEARCH ITEMS CAN YOU FIND?

1. compass
2. canteen
3. map
4. notebook
5. rock hammer

BRACHIOSAURUS

(brak-ee-oh-sawr-us)

154 TO 153 MILLION YEARS AGO

Food: Herbivore • Size: 40 feet tall • Family: Sauropoda
Home: Prehistoric North America, in what is now Colorado and Wyoming

In Jurassic Colorado, a huge dinosaur finally appears. The setting sun makes the dinosaur's scales look orange and purple. From its toes to the top of its head, it stands over 40 feet in the air.

"Why is this one called the 'arm lizard?'" Mateo asks.

"When *Brachiosaurus* was discovered a hundred years ago," Ava says, "one of the only parts paleontologists found was a really big arm!"

Moving closer to some conifer trees, the *Brachiosaurus* eats a mouthful of leaves and branches, swallowing it whole before taking another bite.

"That sure is high up," Ava says, looking at the dinosaur's head in the trees.

"*Brachiosaurus* was definitely one of the tallest dinosaurs," Mateo agrees. "Scientists think it's because there were other long-necked dinosaurs in the same place. All of them needed food!

"That's a long way up to get some salad," Ava says.

HOW MANY OF THE SEARCH ITEMS CAN YOU FIND?

1. watch
2. map
3. *Brachiosaurus* vertebra
4. rock hammer
5. notebook
6. compass

CRETACEOUS PERIOD

145 TO 66 MILLION YEARS AGO

"Let's do this one together!" Ava says, as they press the time machine button. "Yeah! T. rex here we come!"

"Well, let's not rush," Mateo smiles. "The *Tyrannosaurus rex* lived at the very end of the Cretaceous. There are lots of dinosaurs to see!"

"True!" Ava agrees. "Part of the reason there were so many cool dinosaurs during this period is the continents were still drifting apart. North America and Eurasia split, and Africa, South America, and Antarctica all broke up, too."

"That's right!" Mateo adds. "And India was an island until it crashed into Asia!"

"I guess all that moving around gave dinosaurs new places to live," Ava says. "And there are some new plants, too. Like flowers! The oldest flowering plants are about 125 million years old and grew in ancient China."

"Maybe we should get the dinosaurs a bouquet," Mateo says.

"They'd probably just eat it," Ava giggles.

The time machine rumbles and whooshes into the new time period. "We should make sure we get back before the end of the Cretaceous Period," Mateo gulps.

"That's right," Ava nods. "A really big asteroid struck the Earth 66 million years ago. It caused a big extinction and most dinosaurs disappeared. We don't want to become fossils, too!"

UTAHRAPTOR

(you-tah-rap-tor)

126 MILLION YEARS AGO

Food: **Carnivore** • Size: **30 feet long** • Family: **Dromaeosauridae**
Home: **Prehistoric North America, in what is now Utah**

Beneath the shade, a mama *Utahraptor* rests while her babies play. The babies are small, about as big as Ava and Mateo. The mama is almost 20 feet long, and more muscular. All of them are covered in brightly colored feathers.

"I wonder what all those feathers are for!" Mateo exclaims.

"Feathers aren't just for flying," Ava says. "They keep dinosaurs warm, allow them to communicate with friends, or even help them catch their dinner."

"How does that work?" Mateo asks.

"Same as hawks!" Ava explains. "When a *Utahraptor* catches food, they flap their wings to help keep their grip."

"That's cool," Mateo says, "especially with that big claw!"

"It looks a little bit like a cat's claw," Ava says. "But it's way stronger than my kitten's."

HOW MANY OF THE SEARCH ITEMS CAN YOU FIND?

1. compass
2. binoculars
3. *Utahraptor* claw
4. map

5. watch
6. rock hammer
7. mammal *Cifelliodon*

OURANOSAURUS

(oar-an-oh-sawr-us)

125 TO 112 MILLION YEARS AGO

Food: Herbivore • Size: 27 feet long • Family: Ornithopoda
Home: Prehistoric Africa, in what is now Niger

Ava squints through her binoculars at a shape in the distance. "What do you think it is, Mateo?"

"Hmm. It has a big sail . . ." Mateo replies. On the dinosaur's back is a tall, thin structure. Skin is wrapped around long bones on the reptile's back.

"Maybe it's a *Spinosaurus*?" Ava guesses. "That dinosaur has a big sail. But if it is, we should move—that one eats meat!"

"Now I see," Mateo says. "It's an *Ouranosaurus*!"

Sure enough, a big duck-billed dinosaur walks toward them across the mud. The dinosaur has a shovel-shaped beak and spiky thumbs.

"*Ouranosaurus* means 'brave monitor lizard,'" Mateo says. "Paleontologists found its bones in 1962, in the middle of the desert in Niger."

"That's millions of years from now," Ava says. "Let's watch it eat!"

HOW MANY OF THE SEARCH ITEMS CAN YOU FIND?

1. rock hammer
2. notebook
3. *Ouranosaurus* thumb spike
4. binoculars
5. watch
6. compass

VELOCIRAPTOR

(vel-oss-ee-rap-tor)

75 TO 71 MILLION YEARS AGO

Food: Carnivore • Size: About 6 feet long • Family: Dromaeosauridae
Home: Prehistoric China and Mongolia, a place filled with vast sand dunes

"It's so little!" Mateo says.

In front of the explorers, a feathery *Velociraptor* walks along a sand dune in prehistoric Mongolia. The dinosaur is about the size of a turkey and leaves two-toed footprints.

"They're not quite as big as they seem in the movies," Ava chuckles. "But they're still smart predators!"

"How do we know that?" Mateo asks.

"Well, a very special fossil formed when a *Velociraptor* and a *Protoceratops* were stuck together,"

Ava says. "The raptor had its claws stuck on the *Protoceratops*, and the *Protoceratops* was biting the raptor!"

The *Velociraptor* stops and tilts its head. In a flash it pounces at something beneath the sand. A lizard! The *Velociraptor* throws the reptile into the air and catches it with its sharp teeth.

"Looks like it's just smaller snacks today," Mateo says. "That reminds me, I feel hungry enough to eat a *Supersaurus*!"

HOW MANY OF THE SEARCH ITEMS CAN YOU FIND?

1. rock hammer
2. map
3. *Velociraptor* claw
4. binoculars
5. watch
6. notebook
7. compass

MOSASAURUS

(moe-sa-sawr-us)

70 TO 66 MILLION YEARS AGO

Food: Apex predator • **Size:** Up to 56 feet long • **Family:** Mosasauridae
Home: Oceans off the coast of prehistoric Europe and North America

"A sea monster!" Mateo yells. The time machine gently rocks on the waves of the Cretaceous Sea. A little bump makes Ava and Mateo grab the side.

"There's only one reptile this big in this ocean," Ava says. "A *Mosasaurus!*"

"It looks like a big monitor lizard," Ava observes.

"That's because they're related," Mateo says. "*Mosasaurus* isn't a dinosaur. It's a big lizard related to today's Komodo dragons."

The reptile dives beneath the surface again. "I wonder what it eats," Mateo says.

Just then, ammonites (cousins of today's squid) came into view. The *Mosasaurus* opened its jaw, grabbing one as it zipped by.

"I bet *Mosasaurus* would like calamari," Ava chuckles.

HOW MANY OF THE SEARCH ITEMS CAN YOU FIND?

1. compass
2. *Mosasaurus* tooth
3. binoculars
4. watch
5. clam
6. ammonite shell
7. canteen

TRICERATOPS

(try-ser-ah-tops)

68 TO 66 MILLION YEARS AGO

Food: Herbivore • Size: 30 feet long • Family: Ceratopsidae
Home: Prehistoric North America, from Colorado to Alberta

A loud crack sounds through the forest. Ava and Mateo jump. Then it comes again. Crack!

Out in the clearing, two *Triceratops* lock their horns and shove each other. Their feet scrape the mud as they snort and push.

"Wow, those are some stubborn dinosaurs!" Ava says.

"Yeah!" Mateo agrees. "I wonder which one will win?"

"At least we don't have to worry about them eating us," Ava says. "*Triceratops* only eat plants. They have special rows of up to 40 teeth to chew tough plants!

Do you know what else makes the *Triceratops* so special?" she asks. "For starters, it has a frill—a big shield of bone behind its head!"

"That's right!" Mateo agrees. "*Triceratops* means 'three-horned face.' The shape of their horns changes as they grow up. Horns get bigger and curve backward when the dinosaurs are teenagers. They point forward when they're all grown-up."

Ava looks at the two *Triceratops* wrestling in the mud. "They have some growing to do."

HOW MANY OF THE SEARCH ITEMS CAN YOU FIND?

---

1. compass
2. binoculars
3. watch

4. notebook
5. magnolia flower

PACHYCEPHALOSAURUS

(pack-ee-seff-ah-low-sawr-us)

68 TO 66 MILLION YEARS AGO

Food: Herbivore • Size: 14 feet long • Family: Pachycephalosauridae
Home: Prehistoric North America, in what is now Montana and Wyoming

"Now that dinosaur looks like a rock star," Mateo says, pointing at a shape in the forest. It's a *Pachycephalosaurus*, one of the dome-headed dinosaurs that lived in Cretaceous Montana.

The dinosaur walks on two legs and lowers its head to nibble a few leaves.

This gives Ava and Mateo a great view of the dinosaur's spiky head. Around a large bump of bone there are many sharp points on the dinosaur's snout and behind its head.

"I wonder why this dinosaur has a head shaped like a bowling ball," Mateo says.

Ava nods and says, "That's a good question! Some paleontologists think the head shape helps them recognize each other. Others think they also used their heads to fight each other—pow!" Ava knocks her hands together like two colliding bowling balls.

"That must have hurt," Mateo says as he rubs his head. "I guess even dinosaurs got headaches!"

HOW MANY OF THE SEARCH ITEMS CAN YOU FIND?

1. watch
2. magnolia flower
3. beetle
4. rock hammer
5. map
6. compass
7. dinosaur toe bone

TYRANNOSAURUS REX

(tie-ran-oh-sawr-us rex)

68 TO 66 MILLION YEARS AGO

Food: **Apex predator** • Size: **Up to 40 feet long** • Family: **Tyrannosauridae**
Home: **Prehistoric western North America**

The enormous carnivore is curled up with its chin on its tail, snoozing. "How close do you think we can get?" Ava asks.

"I think this is a good place to stop. We can even smell it from here. Pee-ew!" Mateo says.

"Carnivores are definitely a little stinky. What do you think it's been eating?" Ava asks.

"There's lots to eat in prehistoric Montana," Mateo says. "There's *Triceratops, Edmontosaurus,* smaller dinosaurs like *Pachycephalosaurus* . . . the *T. rex* is an apex predator, so it can eat whatever it wants!" Mateo says. The giant dinosaur's eye pops open and it lifts its head. The *Tyrannosaurus* yawns, showing its banana-sized teeth. It stands and stalks something in the forest.

It's a duck-billed dinosaur, an *Edmontosaurus,* that has gotten separated from its herd.

The *T. rex* pounces and misses the duckbill's tail. The *Edmontosaurus* honks and rears up on its hind legs to run away. It's faster than the *T. rex.*

"Did you see that?!" Ava and Mateo say together. The *T. rex* turns to look at them.

"You know, I think it's a good time to go home!" Mateo says.

HOW MANY OF THE SEARCH ITEMS CAN YOU FIND

1. compass
2. binoculars
3. watch
4. notebook
5. rock hammer
6. canteen

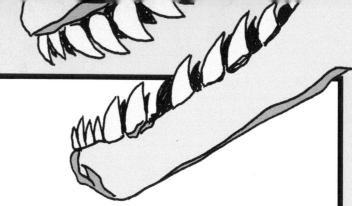

BACK HOME

The time machine hums as the numbers on the console start counting to the present—65 million years ago, 64, 63 . . .

"I can't believe we got to see a *Velociraptor*!" Ava says. "They're so beautiful."

"And *Stegosaurus*!" Mateo exclaims. "I liked the spikes."

"I wish they were still around," Ava says, watching the time ticker zoom toward the present.

"They still are," Mateo says. "*Tawa* and *Triceratops* might not be alive anymore, but we can see their bones at home. We can learn a lot from fossils, too!"

"And there are probably some dinosaurs we don't even know about yet!" Ava says. "When paleontologists find a new one, maybe we can go back and see it."

"Deal!" Mateo says.

The time machine starts the final countdown. Five million years ago, four, three, two, one . . . The doors open up to the present, where new discoveries await.

ANSWERS

Plateosaurus, pages 12–13

Tawa, pages 14–15

Caelestiventus, pages 16–17

Dilophosaurus, pages 20–21

Plesiosaurus, pages 22–23

Megalosaurus, pages 24–25

Stegosaurus, pages 26–27

Brachiosaurus, pages 28–29

Utahraptor, pages 32–33

Ouranosaurus, pages 34–35

Velociraptor, pages 36–37

Mosasaurus, pages 38–39

Triceratops, pages 40–41

Pachycephalosaurus, pages 42–43

Tyrannosaurus Rex, pages 44–45

GLOSSARY

Allosaurus: A large, meat-eating dinosaur that lived in North America and western Europe during the Late Jurassic

Apatosaurus: A large, long-necked, plant-eating dinosaur that lived in North America during the Late Jurassic

Apex predator: A carnivore that has few competitors for food and is not food for other meat-eaters

Araucarioxylon: An extinct species of conifer tree that grew in Triassic forests

Belemnite: A prehistoric squid with a hard shell inside

Brachiosaurus: A large, long-necked, plant-eating dinosaur that lived in North America during the Late Jurassic and is recognizable by its long arms

Brachyphyllum: An extinct conifer with a frond-like shape that grew all over the world during the Age of Dinosaurs

Caelestiventus: A flying reptile called a pterosaur that lived in the Early Jurassic of North America

Carnivore: An animal that eats flesh, either by catching prey or scavenging carcasses

Ceratopsidae: A family of large, horned dinosaurs that includes *Triceratops* and its close relatives

Ceratosaurus: A horned, carnivorous dinosaur that lived in North America during the Late Jurassic

Cifelliodon: A small, badger-like mammal that lived in the Early Cretaceous of North America

Conifer: Woody trees that include pines and their close relatives; often have needles or scale-like leaves

Cretaceous Period: A division of time between 145 and 66 million years ago, starting after the Jurassic

Cycad: An ancient group of plants with a tough, woody trunk and frond-like leaves growing from the top

Deinonychus: A small carnivorous dinosaur with sickle claws on each foot that lived in the Early Cretaceous of North America

Dilophosaurus: A medium-size, carnivorous dinosaur that lived in the Early Jurassic of North America, and is recognizable by the two crests on its head

Dimorphodontid: A group of early pterosaurs, or flying reptiles, with needle-like teeth

Dromaeosauridae: The family of "raptor" dinosaurs that include species like *Velociraptor*

Edmontosaurus: A large, shovel-beaked, herbivorous dinosaur that lived in western North America during the Late Cretaceous

Gigantspinosaurus: A large, armored dinosaur with impressive shoulder spikes that lived in the Late Jurassic of Asia

Ginkgo: An ancient family of trees that thrived in the Mesozoic but has only one living species today

Giraffatitan: A large, long-necked, plant-eating dinosaur that lived in the Late Jurassic of Africa and is related to *Brachiosaurus*

Gorgosaurus: A large, meat-eating dinosaur that lived in the Late Cretaceous of North America and is related to *Tyrannosaurus rex*

Herbivore: An animal that mostly or only eats plants

Insectivore: An animal that mostly or only eats insects

Invertebrate: A huge family of animals defined by their lack of backbone, including worms, insects, and squid

Jurassic Period: A division of time between 201 and 145 million years ago, between the Triassic and Cretaceous

Kentrosaurus: A spiky, armored dinosaur that lived in the Late Jurassic of Tanzania and is related to *Stegosaurus*

Komodo dragon: The world's largest lizard, part of a group called monitor lizards, that are related to the extinct *Mosasaurus*

Laurasia: A prehistoric supercontinent primarily consisting of ancient Europe, Asia, and North America

Lythronax: A large, meat-eating dinosaur that lived in the Late Cretaceous of North America and is related to *Tyrannosaurus rex*

Megalosaurus: A large, meat-eating dinosaur that lived in the Middle Jurassic of Europe and was the first dinosaur to get a scientific name

Mesozoic Era: A division of time that includes the Triassic, Jurassic, and Cretaceous, stretching from 252 to 66 million years ago

Mosasaurus: A huge lizard that lived in the sea during the Late Cretaceous, and is related to today's monitor lizards

Osteoderms: Bones that grow inside the skin, like the armor of an alligator or the plates on the back of *Stegosaurus*

Ouranosaurus: A large, shovel-beaked dinosaur that lived in Africa during the Early Cretaceous, and is recognizable by the sail on its back

Pachycephalosauridae: A family of plant-eating, dome-headed dinosaurs that includes *Pachycephalosaurus*

Pachycephalosaurus: A large, plant-eating dinosaur from the Late Cretaceous of North America that is immediately recognizable by its dome-shaped skull

Pangaea: A prehistoric supercontinent that included all the world's major continents, before breaking up

Piscivore: An animal that mostly or only eats fish

Plateosaurus: A large, long-necked, plant-eating dinosaur that walked on two legs and lived in the Triassic of Europe

Plesiosaurus: A marine reptile with a long neck that lived in the ocean during the Jurassic

Prehistoric: A word referring to anything before the beginning of written human history, generally marked as any time older than 10,000 years ago

Pterosaurs: A family of flying reptiles that were related to dinosaurs, and recognizable by wings made of skin stretched over long finger bones

Sauropoda: A family of large, long-necked dinosaurs that ate plants and walked on all fours

Sauropodomorpha: A family of herbivorous dinosaurs that includes sauropods like Brachiosaurus as well as their close relatives, like Plateosaurus

Spinosaurus: A large, carnivorous dinosaur that lived in Cretaceous Africa and had a large sail on its back

Stegosaurus: A large, armored, plant-eating dinosaur that lived in the Late Jurassic of North America and is recognizable by the plates on its back

Stygimoloch: A medium-size, plant-eating dinosaur with a dome on its head, thought by experts to be the juvenile form of *Pachycephalosaurus*

Supersaurus: A large, long-necked dinosaur related to Diplodocus and could grow to over 100 feet long

Tawa: A small, meat-eating dinosaur that lived in the Triassic of North America

Tethys Sea: A prehistoric ocean that existed for most of the Age of Dinosaurs between the northern and southern continents

Theropod: A family of dinosaurs that walked on two legs and included species like *Tyrannosaurus rex* (many ate meat, but not all of them did)

Torvosaurus: A huge, meat-eating dinosaur that lived in the Late Jurassic of North America and western Europe, recognizable by the long claws on its hands

Triassic Period: A division of time between 252 and 201 million years ago, before the Jurassic

Triceratops: A huge, plant-eating, horned dinosaur that lived in North America during the Late Cretaceous, recognizable by the three horns on its face

Tyrannosauridae: A family of large, meat-eating dinosaurs that includes species like *Gorgosaurus* and *Tyrannosaurus rex*

Tyrannosaurus rex: A huge, meat-eating dinosaur that lived in North America during the Late Cretaceous, recognizable by the two fingers on each hand

Utahraptor: A large, meat-eating dinosaur with a sickle claw on each foot that lived in the Early Cretaceous of North America

Velociraptor: A small, meat-eating dinosaur with a sickle claw on each foot that lived in the Late Cretaceous of Asia

Vertebra: One of the bones of the spine, often with a round central part and more complicated wings of bone on top

RILEY BLACK is a paleontologist and professional science writer. In addition to blogging for *Scientific American*, they are the author of the children's book *Prehistoric Predators*, as well as *Skeleton Keys*, *My Beloved Brontosaurus*, and *Written in Stone* for adults. They live in Salt Lake City, Utah.

SCOTT KOBLISH is a cartoonist and artist who has drawn hundreds of comic books for Marvel and DC Comics. He is a very enthusiastic dinosaur fan and has gone to many museums across the US and Canada in search of dinosaur exhibits; perhaps you have gone to some of the same ones that Scott has! He lives in Los Angeles with his beautiful fiancé and his child.

CPSIA information can be obtained
at www.ICGtesting.com
Printed in the USA
BVHW060422081020
590439BV00005B/6